Christmas Treasures

A Keepsake Collection for the Holidays

Christmas Treasures

Hallmark Editions

Photograph by Jim Cozad

Editorial Research: Barbara Loots and Aileene Neighbors
Book Design and Calligraphy: Rick Cusick

'Tis the season of kindling the fire
of hospitality in the hall,
the genial fire of charity in the heart.
WASHINGTON IRVING

Christmas Bells

I heard the bells on Christmas Day
Their old, familiar carols play,
   And wild and sweet
   The words repeat
Of peace on earth, good will to men!

And thought how, as the day had come,
The belfries of all Christendom
   Had rolled along
   The unbroken song
Of peace on earth, good will to men!

Till, ringing, singing on its way,
The world revolved from night to day,
   A voice, a chime,
   A chant sublime
Of peace on earth, good will to men!
     Henry Wadsworth Longfellow

The Choice

We chose it early with the utmost care,
Then marked it well while nutting in the fall;
And while the autumn fruits were garnered in,
Our fond dreams saw it standing in the hall;
And when at last, the great day drawing near,
With anxious axe, we cut the sturdy tree
From snow and leaves, and proudly bore it home,
Our hearts beating with Christmas ecstasy.

So often since then I have chosen trees
From stores, that are more beautiful I know.
Each time I pick the fairest of them all,
I am reminded of the long ago.
Though choice was small, the memories are best
Of those brought from the woods across the snow.
     Charlotte Carpenter

A Birthday Gift

What can I give Him,
Poor as I am?
If I were a shepherd
I would bring a lamb,
If I were a Wise Man,
I would do my part,
Yet what I can I give Him, –
Give my heart.
Christina Rossetti

Illustration by Arlene Noel

THE NIGHT BEFORE CHRISTMAS

Clement Clarke Moore

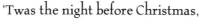

'Twas the night before Christmas,
　　　　　when all through the house
Not a creature was stirring, not even a mouse;
The stockings were hung by the chimney with care,
In hopes that St. Nicholas soon would be there;
The children were nestled all snug in their beds,
While visions of sugar-plums danced in their heads;
And Mamma in her kerchief, and I in my cap,
Had just settled our brains for a long winter's nap,
When out on the lawn there arose such a clatter,
I sprang from my bed to see what was the matter.
Away to the window I flew like a flash,
Tore open the shutters and threw up the sash.
The moon, on the breast of the new-fallen snow,
Gave a luster of mid-day to objects below;
When, what to my wondering eyes should appear,
But a miniature sleigh, and eight tiny reindeer,
With a little old driver, so lively and quick,
I knew in a moment it must be St. Nick.
More rapid than eagles his coursers they came,
And he whistled, and shouted, and called them by name:
"Now, Dasher! now, Dancer! now, Prancer and Vixen!
On, Comet! on, Cupid! on, Donder and Blitzen!
To the top of the porch, to the top of the wall!
Now, dash away, dash away, dash away, all!"
As dry leaves that before the wild hurricane fly,
When they meet with an obstacle, mount to the sky,
So, up to the house-top the coursers they flew,
With a sleigh full of toys— and St. Nicholas, too.

And then in a twinkling I heard on the roof
The prancing and pawing of each little hoof.
As I drew in my head, and was turning around,
Down the chimney St. Nicholas came with a bound.
He was dressed all in fur from his head to his foot,
And his clothes were all tarnished with ashes and soot;
His droll little mouth was drawn up like a bow,
And the beard on his chin was as white as the snow.
The stump of a pipe he held tight in his teeth,
And the smoke it encircled his head like a wreath;
A bundle of toys he had flung on his back,
And he looked like a peddler just opening his pack.
His eyes how they twinkled! his dimples how merry!
His cheeks were like roses, his nose like a cherry;
He had a broad face and a little round belly
That shook when he laughed, like a bowl full of jelly.
He was chubby and plump— a right jolly old elf;
And I laughed when I saw him, in spite of myself.
A wink of his eye, and a twist of his head,
Soon gave me to know I had nothing to dread.
He spoke not a word, but went straight to his work,
And filled all the stockings; then turned with a jerk
And laying his finger aside of his nose,
And giving a nod, up the chimney he rose.
He sprang to his sleigh, to his team gave a whistle,
And away they all flew like the down of a thistle;
But I heard him exclaim ere he drove out of sight,

"HAPPY CHRISTMAS TO ALL,
AND TO ALL A GOOD NIGHT!"

Everywhere, Christmas Tonight

Everywhere — everywhere, Christmas tonight!
Christmas in lands of the Fir tree and Pine,
Christmas in lands of the Palm tree and Vine,
Christmas where snow peaks stand solemn and white,
Christmas where cornfields lie sunny and bright,
Everywhere, everywhere, Christmas tonight!

Phillips Brooks

The Old Country Church

Among my favorite memories
Each year on Christmas Day
Is that old-fashioned country church
Where once I went to pray.
Families came from far and near,
Despite the wintry weather,
To fill the little country church
And worship there together.
Though I have journeyed far
Along the road of life since then,
How often I have longed to be
In that old church again
To share with all my loved ones
The joy of Christmas Day
In that old-fashioned country church
Where once I went to pray.

Edward Cunningham

Christmas Is Love

Christmas is the harvesting of love. Souls are drawn to
other souls. All that we have read and thought and
hoped comes to fruition at this happy time. Our spirits
are astir. We feel within us a strong desire to serve. A
strange, subtle force, a new kindness, animates man
and child. A new spirit is growing in us. No longer are
we content to relieve pain, to sweeten sorrow, to give
the crust of charity. We dare to give friendship, service,
the equal loaf of bread...and love.

Helen Keller

Photograph by Sam Zarember

Illustration by Robert Schneeberg

THE INN KEEPER

Yes, they came to my inn at Bethlehem, and how well I remember the couple; it seems but yesterday. He was a manly sort of man, the kind that would cause you to look again if you saw him once. Kindly and dignified, with long beard, a strong man with quiet manners. There was something that charmed me about the woman who was with him, and — well, I just can't tell you — anyway, one could see that she might soon become a mother. It rather worried me that I didn't have a place for them, but so many had come for the registration, you know. Sanballat, rich merchant, had come down from Damascus; Thaddeus, one of my old customers, had come up from Gaza. A party from Hebron came just at nightfall, and since I knew them all I could not turn them away. Joseph told me that he was from Nazareth, up in the hill country of Galilee. He thought, of course, he could have a place to stay, and as he asked me he looked toward Mary, and knew that I would understand.

I did understand, and I tried to think which of the men I should ask to move and make place for the couple. But how could I ask these customers of mine to inconvenience themselves? After all, I did not know Joseph and Mary. I said to myself, O well, somebody will look after them; I must not disturb the others, and it is a beautiful star-lit night. Here I have it, finally I said to myself, we can make room for them in the manger, and someway they will get along. I have wondered a lot about them since they have gone. He was a manly sort of man, with his long beard, and dignified look, and quiet manners. And the woman, she was like a princess. I wish now that I had said to the men in my inn, we must make a place for this man and this woman from Galilee! But I didn't, and I am sorry. They might, after all, have been people of consequence.

Oliver M. Keve

Currier + Ives

There were nearly 7,000 different Currier and Ives prints published from 1835 to 1907. The prints were lithographed from oil paintings, pen-and-inks, and wash drawings. Some were in black and white; others were in color (usually lithographed in one color and hand colored later). One print was often the work of several artists.

THE ROAD - WINTER

WINTER MOONLIGHT

WINTER IN THE COUNTRY

THE FARMER'S HOME - WINTER

Joyous Announcing

A holly wreath
  upon the door,
A candle
  sending light
From your house,
  from our house;
And running through
  the night
Sound of happy
  greetings,
Of carols,
  sweet and clear —
All with joy
  announcing,
Christmastime
  is here!
Katherine Edelman

Deck the Halls

TRADITIONAL

OLD WELSH AIR

1. Deck the halls with boughs of hol - ly, Fa la la la la, la la la la.
   'Tis the sea - son to be jol - ly, Fa la la la la, la la la la.

2. See the blaz - ing Yule be - fore us, Fa la la la la, la la la la.
   Strike the harp and join the cho - rus, Fa la la la la, la la la la.

Don we now our gay ap - par - el, Fa la la la la la la,
Fol - low me in mer - ry meas - ure, Fa la la la la la la,

Troll the an - cient Yule - tide car - ol, Fa la la la la, la la la la.
While we sing of Yule - tide treas - ure, Fa la la la la, la la la la.

Silent Night

STILLE NACHT

Joseph Mohr

Franz Gruber

1. Si - lent night! Ho - ly night! All is calm, all is bright Round yon
2. Si - lent night! Ho - ly night! Shep-herds quake at the sight, Glo - ries
3. Si - lent night! Ho - ly night! Son of God, love's pure light, Ra - diant

Vir - gin Moth-er and Child! Ho - ly In-fant, so ten-der and mild,
stream from heav-en a - far, Heav'n-ly hosts sing Al - le - lu - ia;
beams from Thy ho - ly face, With the dawn of re - deem - ing grace,

Sleep in heav - en - ly peace. Sleep in heav - en - ly peace.
Christ, the Sav - iour, is born! Christ, the Sav - iour, is born!
Je - sus, Lord, at Thy birth! Je - sus, Lord, at Thy birth.

O Little Town of Bethlehem

ST. LOUIS

PHILLIPS BROOKS

LEWIS H. REDNER

1. O lit - tle town of Beth-le-hem, How still we see thee lie; A - bove thy deep and
2. For Christ is born of Ma - ry; And gath-ered all a - bove, While mor-tals sleep, the
3. How si - lent-ly, how si-lent-ly, The wond-rous gift is giv'n! So God im-parts to
4. O ho - ly Child of Beth-le-hem, De-scend to us we pray; Cast out our sin and

dream-less sleep The si - lent stars go by: Yet in thy dark streets shin-eth The
an - gels keep Their watch of wond-'ring love. O morn-ing stars, to - geth-er Pro-
hu - man hearts The bless-ings of His heav'n. No ear may hear His com-ing, But
en - ter in; Be born in us to - day. We hear the Christ-mas an-gels The

ev - er-last-ing Light; The hopes and fears of all the years Are met in thee to-night.
claim the ho - ly birth; And prais-es sing to God the King, And peace to men on earth.
in this world of sin, Where meek souls will re-ceive Him still, The dear Christ en-ters in.
great glad ti-dings tell; O come to us, a-bide with us, Our Lord Em-man-u - el.

Hark! The Herald Angels Sing

MENDELSSOHN

CHARLES WESLEY

FELIX MENDELSSOHN

1. Hark! The her - ald an - gels sing, "Glo - ry to the new - born King!
2. Christ, by high - est heav'n a - dored, Christ, the ev - er - last - ing Lord!
3. Hail, the heav'n-born Prince of Peace! Hail, the Sun of Right-eous-ness!

Peace on earth, and mer - cy mild; God and sin - ners rec - on - ciled".
Long de - sired, be - hold Him come, Find - ing here His hum - ble home.
Light and life to all He brings, Ris'n with heal - ing in His wings.

Joy - ful, all ye na - tions rise; Join the tri - umph of the skies;
Veiled in flesh the God-head see, Hail th'in-car-nate De - i - ty!
Let us then with an - gels sing, "Glo - ry to the new-born King!

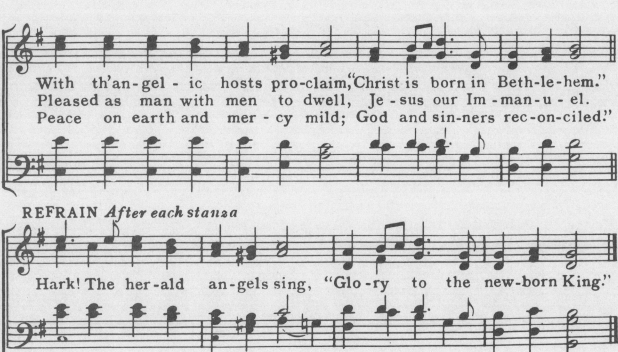

With th'an-gel - ic hosts pro-claim, "Christ is born in Beth-le-hem."
Pleased as man with men to dwell, Je - sus our Im-man-u - el.
Peace on earth and mer - cy mild; God and sin-ners rec-on-ciled."

REFRAIN *After each stanza*

Hark! The her-ald an-gels sing, "Glo-ry to the new-born King."

Jingle Bells

fun it is to ride and sing   A sleigh-ing song to-night!
got in-to a drift-ed bank, And we, we got up-sot.
hitch him to an o-pen sleigh, And crack! you'll take the lead.

REFRAIN

Jin-gle Bells! Jin-gle Bells! Jin-gle all the way! Oh, what fun it is to ride

1
In a   one-horse o-pen sleigh!

2
In a one-horse o-pen sleigh!

Winter Music

Now under paler sun
The leafless tree
Crusted from night
With winter ice and snow
Makes bell-like music,
As with morning breeze,
Bare fingers, winter-dark
Move to and fro…
Like harpist touching
Waiting strings at will,
Small chimes replacing
Summer notes now still.

Katherine Edelman

Star Silver

The silver of one star
Plays cross-lights against pine green.

And the play of this silver
Crosswise against the green
Is an old story...
                    thousands of years.

And sheep raisers on the hills by night
Watching the wooly four- footed ramblers,
Watching a single silver star —
Why does the story never wear out?

And a baby slung in a feed-box
Back in a barn in a Bethlehem slum,
A baby's first cry mixed with the crunch
Of a mule's teeth on Bethlehem Christmas corn,
Baby fists softer than snowflakes of Norway,
The vagabond Mother of Christ
And the vagabond men of wisdom,
All in a barn on a winter night,
And a baby there in swaddling clothes on hay —
Why does the story never wear out?

The sheen of it all
Is a star silver and a pine green
For the heart of a child asking a story,
The red and hungry, red and hankering heart
Calling for cross- lights of silver and green.
                    Carl Sandburg

Ornaments

The ornaments upon our tree
Have secrets of their own
Of other trees and Christmases
That each of them has known.
The chipped ones hung upon our trees
Before the children came;
The elves were bought for our first son
Who gave them each a name;
Our daughter made the paper rings
When she was only three;
And we all picked out the angel
That crowns our Christmas tree.
They're all different shapes and colors,
But I know and love them all,
And if they could only speak,
What joys they could recall!
                    Kay Andrew

Photograph by Richard Fanolio

The Juggler's Christmas Gift

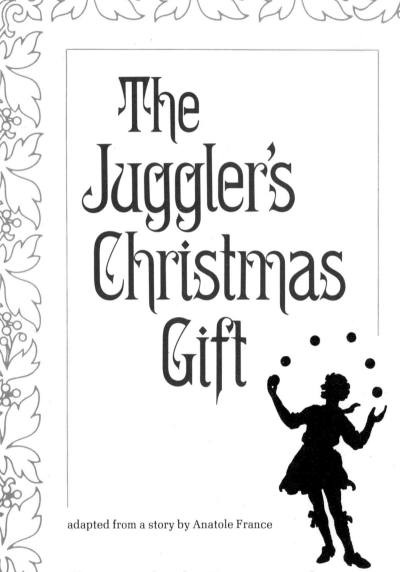

adapted from a story by Anatole France

There once lived in France a wandering juggler named Barnaby. When he came to a village square where he wished to perform, he started his act by balancing a tin plate on the tip of his nose. After that trick he stood on his hands, throwing six copper balls into the air and catching them with his feet. Next, he juggled a dozen knives with his head between his knees. Following each trick he came forward and bowed to the crowd that had gathered. They applauded and threw pennies.

Despite his great skill as a juggler, Barnaby was very poor. He suffered most in the winter. It was then that the ground was frozen hard, the weather bad, and the crowds small. Nevertheless, Barnaby was a humble man who loved God.

Early one December evening after a heavy snowstorm, the juggler overtook a monk walking along the road between two villages. Although he was quite cold and hungry, Barnaby greeted the monk cheerfully. The juggler was dressed in his only clothes — the green tunic and tights in which he performed. The monk asked about the garments. "I am a juggler," said Barnaby, "and it would be the best life in the world, if only it provided enough bread to satisfy my hunger."

"Ah, my friend," said the monk, "there is no better life in all the world than serving our Lord."

The juggler and the monk walked in silence for a way before Barnaby replied — "Good father, I spoke too quickly. The life I lead cannot in any way be compared to your calling. There may be joy in balancing a penny on a stick on the tip of my nose, but it has none of the glory of serving God. I would gladly give up juggling to serve God as you do."

The monk looked deeply into the juggler's eyes. He said, "Dear friend, if you truly believe what you say, come with me and you shall serve God in the monastery where I am the abbot."

So Barnaby followed the holy man to his monastery. There, as a monk, he dedicated his life to the service of God. As Christmas approached, the other monks began preparing gifts for the Blessed Virgin Mary. The abbot himself was writing a book dealing with the virtues of the Mother of God. Brother Maurice copied the abbot's writings in beautiful script on sheets of vellum. Brother Alexander adorned the pages with delicate miniature paintings. Brother Marbode spent all his days carving religious figures in stone. Some of the monks were also poets; they composed hymns in Latin. There was even a brother who sang in rhymed verse about the miracles attributed to the help of Our Lady.

Barnaby admired the talents of his fellow monks and marveled at their devotion. His own ignorance and simplicity saddened him.

"Ah, me!" he sighed. "I have no gift to offer the Holy Mother of God. I'm uneducated and unskilled in the fine arts — I cannot write or illustrate books, or sculpture in stone, or compose music, or make rhymes to sing. I am only a miserable fool."

Day by day he was more downcast. Then a wonderful idea came to him. He awakened filled with joy on the day before Christmas and hurried to the chapel. He remained there alone for more than an hour. After the noon meal he went again to the chapel. By this time his sadness vanished completely. In fact, his change in temperament was so remarkable it aroused the curiosity of the other monks.

The abbot decided to investigate. That night — it was Christmas Eve — the abbot and two older monks hid in the chapel to see whether Barnaby might return.

He did. Head bowed, Barnaby walked up the aisle to the altar. Before the statue of Our Lady he carefully laid his juggler's cloth on the stone floor. Silently he began to juggle — first with copper balls, then with spoons and knives. The old monks were dumbfounded. A sacrilege! The abbot, knowing Barnaby to be a devout man, thought the juggler had gone mad.

He and the two older monks started toward the poor fellow to lead him away. Then a strange thing happened. The statue of the Blessed Virgin came to life. And stepping down from the altar, Our Lady wiped the perspiration from the juggler's forehead with the hem of her blue robe.

The abbot and the two older monks fell to their knees. "Truly," said the abbot, "the gift of Barnaby the juggler is the greatest of all! He has given himself."

Christmas Hash
By Ogden Nash

It's time to decorate the tree
And if you're anything like me
When you mix little bulbs and wires
Electricity expires —
Birds and stars become unspangled
Angels in your hair get tangled
And if you laugh off such mishaps
Ladders under you collapse —
But still I know if you're like me
You wouldn't miss it — no sirree !

STEINBERG

Illustration by Saul Steinberg

Tiny reindeer hoofs are drumming,
Listen, Santa Claus is coming!
See his tummy bulge and billow!
That is Mother's favorite pillow.
All her cotton, as she feared,
Has been purloined to make his beard.
Her lipstick sets his cheeks a-glowing,
His chest expands with Ho Ho Hoing.
That last Ho Ho was not too smart—
Santa Claus has come apart!

My fingers ache from lugging parcels,
I limp on battered metatarsals,
My tongue is dry from licking stamps,
I'm lost in Christmas lights and amps,
I'm in that yearly Yuletide mess,
And so are you I shrewdly guess.
It's tough on you and rough on me
But gosh, it's worth it, don't you agree?

STEINBERG

Christmas Eve
Nearing Midnight in New York

The Christmas trees are almost all sold
And the ones that are left go cheap.
The children almost all over town
Have almost gone to sleep.

The skyscraper lights on Christmas Eve
Have almost all gone out.
There's very little traffic,
Almost no one about.

Our town's almost as quiet
As Bethlehem must have been
Before a sudden angel chorus
Sang PEACE ON EARTH!
GOOD WILL TO MEN!

Our old Statue of Liberty
Looks down almost with a smile
As the Island of Manhattan
Awaits the morning of the Child.
Langston Hughes

Welcome, Christmas!

How you change
the rhythm
of our lives!
Now we find the time
for warm words…
small kindnesses…
unhurried chats
and friendly smiles.
You work your magic
in every heart
as all the world
draws close
in celebration!
Barbara Burrow

Snowflakes

Falling all the nighttime,
Falling all the day,
Silent into silence,
From the faraway;
Never came like glory
To the fields and trees,
Never summer blossoms
Thick and white as these.

Falling all the nighttime,
Falling all the day,
Follow, follow, follow,
Fold it soft away;
Folding, folding, folding,
Fold the world away,
Souls of flowers drifting
Down the winter day.
John Vance Cheney

Home

There's no place
   like home at Christmas —
nowhere is joy so abundant . . .
traditions so heartwarming . . .
love so unlimited.
Marjorie Frances Ames

A Christmas Prayer

May we see with the eyes of children again
Those wonderful Christmas sights
That can give so much sleepless excitement
To magical winter nights.

May we love with the hearts of children again,
Without any need to pretend,
Finding in each man a brother,
Being to each man a friend.
Karen Ravn

CHRISTMAS LEGENDS

THE CHRISTMAS WREATH

IN 1444, evergreen boughs were used as Christmas decorations in the streets of London. And in sixteenth-century Germany, branches of fir or spruce were intertwined in a circular shape. This symbolized the love of God, which has no beginning and no ending. The wreath was laid on a table. On each of the four Sundays of Advent, a candle was attached to the wreath.

THE CHRISTMAS TREE

THE CUSTOM of decorating small evergreen trees at Christmas began in Germany. One legend suggests that St. Boniface, the English missionary to Germany in the eighth century, started the custom. He is said to have replaced the pagan worship of a sacred oak with a young evergreen tree adorned to symbolize the new faith.

The Christmas tree arrived in America before it reached England. Hessian soldiers in the employ of George III decorated trees during the American Revolution. And even earlier, German settlers in Pennsylvania were decorating Christmas trees with lights, sweets and colored paper. The Christmas tree became part of the traditional English celebration only after the marriage of the German Prince Albert to Queen Victoria.

THE MISTLETOE

ANCIENT DRUIDS (pagan Celtic priests) believed mistletoe had medicinal powers and was sacred. They thought it brought good fortune. The house in which it hung was magically protected from witchcraft. One early Christian source compares mistletoe to a link between heaven and earth since it grows in trees and never touches the ground. Mistletoe was also considered the plant of peace, and under it enemies in ancient Scandinavia met to reconcile their differences. From this ceremony came the English custom of kissing beneath the mistletoe – the one tradition involving mistletoe that has survived to the present.

Photograph by Maxine Jacobs

...YES, VIRGINIA, THERE IS A SANTA CLAUS.
He exists as certainly as love and generosity
and devotion exist, and you know that they abound
and give to your life its highest beauty and joy.
Alas! how dreary would be the world
if there were no Santa Claus! It would be as dreary
as if there were no Virginias. There would be no child-like faith then,
no poetry, no romance to make tolerable this existence.
We should have no enjoyment, except in sense and sight.
The eternal light with which childhood fills the world would be extinguished....
No Santa Claus? Thank God, he lives and he lives forever.
A thousand years from now, Virginia,
nay, ten times ten thousand years from now,
he will continue to make glad the hearts of childhood.

Frank Church
From an editorial in the *New York Sun*,
Sept. 21, 1897

Santa Claus first appeared illustrated as a "chubby, jolly old elf" in 1863 in <u>Harper's Weekly</u> and a book of Christmas verse.

Santa's most famous portrait artist, a 23-year-old German immigrant named Thomas Nast, was to become one of the great magazine illustrators of his day.

The national popularity of Santa Claus grew with Nast's and with the increasing interest in national magazines. He changed from the Dutch Santa of Washington Irving's "Knickerbocker History" to become the Santa of "The Night Before Christmas" — the fat, jolly Santa of white beard, red suit, and wide leather belt. He became the Santa we know today.

Nast went on to fame as a political cartoonist and the designer of our two political party symbols, the Republican elephant and the Democratic donkey.

THE TWELVE DAYS OF CHRISTMAS

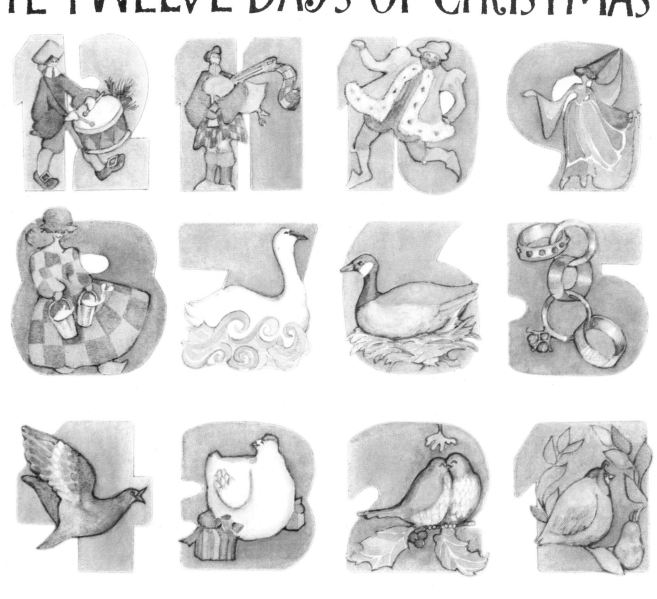

Illustration by Dotty Davidson

THE TWELFTH DAY OF CHRISTMAS
MY TRUE LOVE SENT TO ME
TWELVE DRUMMERS DRUMMING,
ELEVEN PIPERS PIPING,
TEN LORDS A-LEAPING,
NINE LADIES DANCING,
EIGHT MAIDS A-MILKING,
SEVEN SWANS A-SWIMMING,
SIX GEESE A-LAYING,
FIVE GOLD RINGS,
FOUR COLLY BIRDS,
THREE FRENCH HENS,
TWO TURTLE DOVES,
AND A PARTRIDGE IN A PEAR TREE.

A CHRISTMAS CAROL

By Charles Dickens
(adapted for modern readers)

Illustration by Brad Holland

Marley's Ghost

OLD MARLEY was as dead as a doornail. And Scrooge knew it, of course. Scrooge and he had been partners for many years. Yet Scrooge never painted out old Marley's name There it stood, years afterwards, above the warehouse door— Scrooge and Marley. Sometimes people new to the business called Scrooge Scrooge, and sometimes Marley. He answered to both names. It didn't matter to him.

Oh! But Ebenezer Scrooge was stingy! He was a squeezing, wrenching, grasping, clutching old sinner! Nobody ever stopped him in the street to say, "My dear Scrooge, how are you? When will you come to see me?" No beggars asked him for money.

No children asked him what time it was. In fact people seldom talked to him at all. But what did Scrooge care! To be left alone was the very thing he liked.

One Christmas Eve, old Scrooge sat in his office. It was cold, bleak, foggy weather. The city clocks had just struck three, but it was quite dark already.

The door of Scrooge's office was open so that he could keep his eye on his clerk who sat at a tiny desk in the next room copying letters. Scrooge had a very small fire, but the clerk's fire was very much smaller. And he couldn't add more coal, for Scrooge kept the coalbox in his own room; and the clerk knew that if he came in with the shovel, he would be in danger of losing his job. So the clerk put on his white scarf and tried to warm himself by the flickering candle that lighted his work.

"A Merry Christmas, Uncle! God bless you!" cried a cheerful voice. It was Scrooge's nephew who came in just then.

"Bah!" said Scrooge, "humbug!"

"Christmas a humbug, Uncle! You don't mean that!"

"I do. Away with Merry Christmas! What's Christmas time to you but a time for paying bills without money; a time for finding yourself a year older, and not an hour richer. If I had my way, every idiot who goes around with 'Merry Christmas' on his lips would be boiled in his own soup and buried with a stake of holly through his heart. He should!"

"Uncle!"

"Nephew, keep Christmas in your own way, and let me keep it in mine."

"Keep it! But you don't keep it."

"Let me leave it alone, then. It's my business, Nephew, not yours!"

"Don't be angry, Uncle. Come! Have dinner with us tomorrow."

Scrooge said that he would not, and he said it most rudely.

"But why?" cried Scrooge's nephew. "Why?"

"Good afternoon!"

"But, Uncle, you never come to see my wife and me!"

"Good afternoon."

"I want nothing from you; I ask nothing of you; why can't we be friends?"

"Good afternoon."

"I am sorry to find you so stubborn. But I have never quarreled with you, and I'll keep my Christmas humor to the last. So a Merry Christmas, Uncle!"

At closing time Scrooge climbed down from his stool. When the clerk saw him, he quickly snuffed his candle out and put on his hat.

"You want all day off tomorrow, I suppose?"

"If it's all right, sir."

"It's not all right, and it's not fair. If I stopped a day's pay for it, you'd think it was unfair, wouldn't you?"

"Yes, sir."

"And yet you don't think it unfair when I pay a day's wages for no work."

"It's only once a year, sir."

"A poor excuse for picking a man's pocket every twenty-fifth of December! Well, be here all the earlier next morning."

The clerk promised that he would, and Scrooge walked out with a growl. The office was closed in a twinkling. The clerk had no topcoat, so he wrapped the long ends of his white scarf around him and ran home as fast as he could to play with his children.

Scrooge ate his lonely dinner in his usual lonely restaurant. Then he read the newspapers and went home to bed. He lived in a towering building that once belonged to his partner. The building was old and gloomy now, for nobody lived in it but Scrooge.

As he started to unlock the door, Scrooge looked at the knocker that hung on it, and there he saw not a knocker but Marley's face.

It was not angry but looked at Scrooge as Marley used to look — ghostly glasses turned up upon its ghostly forehead.

As Scrooge stared at the face, which had a greenish light about it, it changed back into a knocker again. He said, "pooh, pooh!" and closed the door with a bang.

The sound boomed through the house like thunder. Every room seemed to have an echo of its own. Scrooge was not a man to be frightened by echoes. He locked the door, walked across the hall, and climbed the stairs.

Up Scrooge went, not caring about how dark it was. Darkness is cheap, and Scrooge liked it. But he still remembered the face on the knocker, and before he shut his door, he walked through his rooms to see that everything was all right.

Quite satisfied, he locked and double-locked his door. Then he undressed, put on his nightgown, slippers and nightcap, and sat down to rest before the low fire.

Suddenly he heard a clanking noise, far down below, as if someone were dragging a heavy chain over the cellar floor.

The noise grew much louder and seemed to come from the rooms below; then it came up the stairs and headed straight toward his door.

It came on through the heavy door, and a spirit passed into the room before his eyes. The tiny flame in the fireplace burned brighter, as though it cried, "I know him! Marley's ghost!"

And indeed it was Marley in his pigtail, usual short coat, tights, and boots. His body was so clear that Scrooge could look right through him and see the two buttons on his coat behind. But, though he looked at the ghost and noticed the folded handkerchief wrapped around its head and chin, he still didn't believe it was real.

"Well, now!" said Scrooge, as cold as ever. "What do you want with me?"

"Much!" It was Marley's voice; no doubt about it.

"Who are you?"

"Ask me who I was."

"Who *were* you then?"

"In life I was your partner, Jacob Marley."

"Humbug!"

"You don't believe in me."

"I don't."

"You see me, don't you?"

"Yes."

"Why do you doubt your senses?"

"Because something must be bothering them. A slight disorder of the stomach makes them cheat. You may be an undigested bit of beef, a blot of mustard, a crumb of cheese, a piece of underdone potato. There's more of gravy than of grave about you, whatever you are!"

Scrooge was not in the habit of cracking jokes, nor did he really feel very funny then. The truth is that he was trying to keep Marley from seeing how frightened he was.

But he was frightened much worse when the phantom took the bandage off its head, as if it were too warm to wear indoors, and its lower jaw dropped down upon its breast!

"Mercy! Awful spirit, why do you trouble me? Why do you walk the earth, and why do you come to me?"

"I cannot tell you all I would. I cannot rest, I cannot stay, I cannot linger anywhere. In life I had no time for anything but our business. Hear me! In life my thoughts never left the narrow limits of our office. Now, in death, I must travel far to make up for all the things I should have done. Weary journeys lie before me!"

"Dead for seven years. And traveling all the time! You travel fast?"

"On the wings of the wind."

"But you were always a good man of business, Jacob," Scrooge said.

"Business!" cried the ghost, wringing its hands again. "Mankind was my business. Love for others was my business; charity and mercy were my business!"

Scrooge was so upset to hear the spirit going on like this that he began to shake.

"Hear me! My time is nearly gone."

"I will. But don't be hard on me, Jacob!"

"I am here to warn you that you still have a chance to escape my fate, Ebenezer. You will be haunted by three spirits."

"Is that the chance you mentioned, Jacob? I — I think I'd rather not."

"Without their visits you cannot hope to avoid the path I walk. Expect the first tonight, when the bell tolls one. You will see me no more; but be sure, for your own sake, that you remember what I have told you!"

The spirit walked backward from him; and at every step the window raised itself a little, so when the spirit reached it, it was wide open.

Scrooge closed the window, and examined the door. It was still double-locked. He tried to say "Humbug!" but couldn't quite get it out. Instead he went straight to bed, pulled up the cover, and fell asleep immediately.

The First of the Three Spirits

When Scrooge awoke, it was dark. But as he lay there he heard a church clock strike ONE.

Light flashed up in the room, and the curtains of his bed were pulled aside by a strange figure. Its hair, which hung far down its back, was white like an old man's; and yet the face was smooth like a child's. It held a branch of fresh green holly in its hand; and its clothes were trimmed with summer flowers.

"Are you the spirit, sir, I was told to expect?"

"I am!"

"Who and what are you?"

"I am the Ghost of Christmas Past."

"Long past?"

"No. Your past. We will see shadows of the things that have been, but they will not be able to see or hear us. Rise and walk with me!"

Scrooge wanted to say that the hour was late, the bed was warm, the weather was bitter; that he was dressed only in his slippers, nightgown, and nightcap; and that he had a bad cold. But he didn't think it would do any good. Instead, he climbed out of bed and followed the spirit until it moved toward the window. Then Scrooge became more frightened than ever.

"I am only a man. I'll fall!"

"Touch my hand there," said the spirit, laying it upon his heart. As the words were spoken they passed through the wall and stood on the sidewalk of a busy city. It was plain by the decorations in the shop windows that here, too, it was Christmas time. The ghost stopped at a certain warehouse door, and asked Scrooge if he knew it.

"Know it! I once worked here!"

They went in. There was an old gentleman sitting behind such a high desk that if he had been two inches taller he would have knocked his head against the ceiling. Scrooge cried in excitement: "Why, it's old Fezziwig!"

Old Fezziwig laid down his pen and looked up at the clock. He rubbed his hands, adjusted his waistcoat, laughed all over himself, from his shoes to his belly, and called out in a jolly voice: "Yo ho, there! Ebenezer! Dick!"

A young man, who was Scrooge's former self, hurried into the room with another young man.

"Dick Wilkins!" said Scrooge to the ghost. "My old fellow worker. Dear, dear!"

"Yo ho, my boys!" said Fezziwig. "No more work tonight. Christmas Eve, Dick. Christmas, Ebenezer! Let's have the shades up before a man can say Jack Robinson! Clear away, my lads, and let's have lots of room here!"

Clear away! There was nothing they wouldn't have cleared away for old Fezziwig. Everything movable was packed off, the floor was swept, the lamps were turned up, coal was heaped upon the fire; and the warehouse was as snug and warm and dry and bright a ballroom as you could hope to see on a winter's night.

In came a fiddler with a music book, and he sat at the tall desk. In came Mrs. Fezziwig, smiling happily. In came the three Miss Fezziwigs. In came their boy friends. In came all the young men and women who worked for Fezziwig. In came the housemaid with her cousin the baker. In came the cook with her friend the milkman. In they all came one after another, and away they all danced, down the floor and back again, round and round as the fiddler played. At last old Fezziwig clapped his hands to stop the dance and cried out; "Well done!" The fiddler dried his face and had a cool drink while everyone talked and laughed at once.

Then there were more dances, and there was cake and eggnog, and cold roast beef, and mince pies, and plenty to drink. It was a happy evening, and everyone danced and ate and laughed to his heart's content.

When the clock struck eleven the ball broke up. Mr. and Mrs. Fezziwig stood by the door, and, shaking hands with every person as he or she went out, wishing each a Merry Christmas. When everybody had gone but Ebenezer and Dick, they did the same to them, and the lads then went to their beds which were under a counter in the back shop.

"A small matter," said the ghost, "to make these silly folks so happy. He really hasn't spent much money."

"It isn't that," said Scrooge, still speaking like his former self. "He has the power to make us happy or unhappy, to make our jobs easier or harder. His power lies in being kind and thoughtful, and doing nice things for all who work for him. So you see, the happiness he gives is just as great as if it cost a fortune."

Suddenly he became very tired and found himself back in his own bedroom. He stumbled into bed and immediately sank into a heavy sleep

The Second of the Three Spirits

Scrooge awoke in his own bedroom. There was no doubt about that. But there was a great light coming from his sitting room. He put on his slippers and timidly shuffled in to see what was causing it. The walls and ceiling were so hung with green branches that it looked like a forest, and the merriest blaze roared up the chimney that the old fireplace had known for many and many a winter. Heaped upon the floor, to form a kind of throne, were turkeys, geese, pigs, long strings of sausages, mince pies, plum puddings, barrels of oysters, chestnuts, apples, oranges, pears, huge cakes, and great bowls of punch. Upon this throne sat a smiling giant who held a glowing torch raised high to shed its light on Scrooge as he came peeping round the door.

"Come in — come in and know me better, man! I am the Ghost of Christmas Present. Look at me! You have never seen anyone like me before."

"Never. Spirit, take me where you will. I am ready to learn what you will teach me."

"Touch my robe!"

Scrooge did as he was told. The room and its contents all vanished, and they stood before the house of Scrooge's clerk, Bob Cratchit, on a snowy Christmas morning.

Mrs. Cratchit was dressed poorly in a patched-up gown, but in her hair she wore bright ribbons. She set the table, helped by Belinda Cratchit, second of her daughters, who also wore ribbons in her hair. Master Peter Cratchit wore one of his father's shirts which was much too large for him. And now two smaller Cratchits, boy and girl, came tearing in, screaming that outside the baker's they had smelled the goose, their very own goose! These young Cratchits danced about the table and shouted happily while Peter Cratchit blew the fire under the pan until the potatoes, bubbling up, knocked loudly at the lid to be let out and peeled.

"What is keeping your precious father?" said Mrs. Cratchit. "And your brother, Tiny Tim! And Martha!"

"Here's Martha, Mother!" said a girl who was watching out the window.

"Here's Martha, Mother!" cried the two young Cratchits.

"Hurrah! There's such a goose, Martha!"

"Why, bless your heart, my dear. How late you are!" said Mrs. Cratchit, kissing her a dozen times and taking off her coat and bonnet for her. "But never mind. Now you're here. Sit down before the fire, my dear, and have a warm drink. "

"No, no! There's father coming," cried the two young Cratchits who were everywhere at once. "Hide, Martha, hide!"

So Martha hid herself, and in came Bob, the father, with at least three feet of scarf wrapped around him and his threadbare clothes patched and brushed. Tiny Tim was perched upon his shoulder. Poor Tiny Tim. He held a little crutch, and on his legs he wore an iron brace!

"Why, where's our Martha?" cried Bob Cratchit, looking round.

"Not coming," said Mrs. Cratchit.

"Not coming!" said Bob, suddenly looking very sad. "Not coming on Christmas day!" Then Martha popped out from behind the closet door and ran into his arms while the two young Cratchits carried Tiny Tim off into the kitchen so that he could hear the pudding bubbling in the pan.

"And how did little Tim behave?" asked Mrs. Cratchit when Bob had hugged his daughter to his heart's content.

"As good as gold," said Bob. "Somehow he gets thoughtful, sitting by himself so much. He told me that he hoped people saw him in church because he was a cripple and it might be pleasant for them to remember on Christmas day who made cripples walk and blind men see."

Before another word was spoken, Tiny Tim was brought back by his brother and sister to his stool beside the fire. Bob mixed hot punch, stirred it round and round, and put it by the fire to simmer. Master Peter and the two young Cratchits went after the goose, and they soon returned with it held high for all to see.

Mrs. Cratchit made the gravy hissing hot. Master Peter mashed the potatoes; Miss Belinda sweetened up the applesauce; Martha dusted the plates; and Bob put Tiny Tim beside him at a corner of the table. The two young Cratchits set chairs for everybody; then they scrambled onto their seats and crammed spoons into their mouths to keep from shrieking for goose before their turns came to be served. At last everything was ready, and grace was said. There was a breathless pause as Mrs. Cratchit looked slowly along the carving knife and prepared to plunge it into the goose. But when she did, and when the long expected gush of stuffing popped forth, they all began to talk at once and even Tiny Tim, excited by the two young Cratchits, beat on the table with the handle of his knife, and feebly cried, "Hurrah!"

Bob said he didn't believe there ever was such a goose cooked. Everyone bragged on its tenderness and flavor and size. Indeed, with the applesauce and mashed potatoes, there was enough dinner for the whole family. Mrs. Cratchit looked at one small bite left upon the dish and said with great delight that they hadn't eaten it all at last! But now the plates were changed by Miss Belinda, and Mrs. Cratchit left the room to bring in the pudding. In half a minute she proudly entered with the pudding as firm as a speckled cannon ball, blazing in a tiny measure of brandy and crowned with holly.

"Oh, what a wonderful pudding!" Bob Cratchit said. Everybody had something to say about it, but nobody said or thought it was at all a small pudding for a large family. Any Cratchit would have blushed to hint at such a thing.

At last the dinner was all done, the table was cleared, and the hearth swept. Apples and oranges were put upon the table, and a shovelful of chestnuts on the fire.

Then all the Cratchit family sat around the hearth, and Bob Cratchit served the punch with beaming looks while the chestnuts on the fire spluttered noisily. Then Bob proposed:

"A Merry Christmas to us all, my dears. God bless us!"

Which all the family repeated.

"God bless us every one!" said Tiny Tim, the last of all.

He sat very close to his father's side upon his small stool. Bob held his withered little hand in his as if he dreaded that Tiny Tim might be taken from him.

"Mr. Scrooge!" said Bob, "a toast to Mr. Scrooge!"

Scrooge was surprised to hear his own name.

"Mr. Scrooge, indeed!" cried Mrs. Cratchit. "I wish I had him here. I'd give him a piece of my mind!"

"My dear," said Bob, "the children! Christmas day!"

"I'll drink it for your sake and the day's," said Mrs. Cratchit, "not for his. Long life to him! A Merry Christmas and a Happy New Year! He'll be very merry and very happy, I'm sure!"

The children drank the toast after her, but they only did it to please their father. Tiny Tim drank it last of all. The mention of Scrooge had cast a dark shadow on the party which lasted for a full five minutes.

After it had passed away, they were ten times merrier than before. All this time the chestnuts and the jug of punch went round and round. After a while they had a song from Tiny Tim about a lost child traveling in the snow. He had a clear little voice and sang it very well indeed. There was nothing special about all this. They were not a handsome family; they were not well dressed, their shoes were scuffed, their clothes were scanty. But they were happy and grateful and pleased with one another; and when the room began to fade away, Scrooge had his eye on Tiny Tim until the last.

It surprised Scrooge as this scene disappeared to hear a hearty laugh. It was a much greater surprise to recognize it as his own nephew's and to find himself in a bright room of his nephew's house with the spirit by his side.

When Scrooge's nephew laughed, his wife laughed, too, and they were both joined by their guests who sat around the table with them.

"He said that Christmas was a humbug!" cried Scrooge's nephew. "He believed it too!"

Again they all laughed. "He's a funny old fellow," Scrooge's nephew went on. "He's not as pleasant as he should be, but I have nothing to say against him. He hurts no one but himself. Here he takes it into his head to dislike us, and he won't come to eat with us. So what happens? He misses a fine dinner."

Everybody agreed that the dinner had been perfect, and they all laughed again at Scrooge for having turned down the chance to share it.

After tea they had some music. They were a happy group who loved to sing — especially Topper, who could growl away in a bass voice and never even get red in the face over it.

But they didn't spend the whole evening singing. After a while they played games, for it is good to be children sometimes, especially at Christmas.

"Look," whispered Scrooge, "they're starting. Let's stay a bit longer, Spirit!"

It was a game called "Yes and No" where Scrooge's nephew had to think of something, and the rest must find out what. And he could only answer their questions by a "yes" or a "no." By his answers they learned that he was thinking of an animal, a live animal, rather a disagreeable animal, an animal that growled and grunted sometimes, and talked sometimes, and lived in London, and walked about the streets, and wasn't paid much attention, and wasn't led by anybody, and didn't live in a zoo, and was never killed by a butcher, and was not a horse, or a donkey, or a cow, or a bull, or a tiger, or a dog, or a pig, or a cat, or a bear. At every new question asked him, the nephew burst into a fresh roar of laughter and became so tickled that he had to get up off the sofa and stamp his foot. At last the plump sister cried out,

"I know what it is, Fred! I know what it is!"

"What is it?" cried Fred.

"It's your Uncle Scro-o-o-o-oge!"

Which it certainly was. Everyone laughed and said it had been a fine game. But some of them thought that the reply to "Is it a bear?" ought to have been "Yes."

Suddenly the whole scene changed again, and Scrooge and the spirit were once more upon their travels.

As they stood together in an open place, a church bell rang. Scrooge looked about him for the ghost, but it was gone. He remembered that Jacob Marley had said there would be a third ghost, and lifting up his eyes, he saw a phantom whose face was hidden by a dark hood coming across the ground toward him.

The Last of the Spirits

The phantom moved slowly and silently. When it came near him, Scrooge bent down upon his knee, for this spirit seemed so sad that Scrooge was frightened.

Wrapped around it was a long black robe which covered its head, its face, its body, and left nothing of it visible except one outstretched hand. The spirit neither spoke nor moved.

"Are you the Ghost of Christmas Yet to Come? Ghost of the future! I am more afraid of you than of any spirit I have seen. But I know that you've come to do me good, and I hope to live to be a better man than what I was, so I am ready to go with you gladly. Will you not speak to me?"

It remained silent. The hand was pointed straight before them.

"Lead on! Lead on! The night is almost gone, and we must not lose a moment, I know. Lead on, Spirit!"

They were immediately standing in the heart of the city on Commercial Street among the merchants.

The spirit stopped beside one little group of businessmen. The hand was pointed to them, so Scrooge walked forward to listen to their talk.

"No," said a great fat man with a monstrous chin, "I don't know much about it either way. I only know he's dead."

"When did he die?" asked another.

"Last night, I believe."

"Why, what was the matter with him? I thought he'd never die."

"God knows," said the first with a yawn.

"What has he done with his money?" asked a red-faced gentleman.

"I haven't heard," said the man with the large chin. "His company, perhaps. He hasn't left it to me. That's all I know."

Scrooge was surprised that the spirit should want him to listen to something so unimportant. But he was certain that it must have some hidden purpose. He wondered what it might be. It could have nothing to do with the death of Jacob, his old partner, for that was past, and this was the ghost of the future.

He looked about for himself, but though the clock pointed to his usual time of day for being there, he could not see himself among the crowds that walked up and down the street. This didn't surprise Scrooge, however, for he had already made up his mind to change his way of life. He supposed this to be the reason for his not being in his old place at this hour.

They left the busy street and went into another part of town to a shop where iron, rags, bottles, bones, and greasy rubbish were bought. An old, grey-haired rascal sat smoking his pipe by the doorway. Scrooge and the phantom arrived just as a woman with a heavy bundle slunk into the shop. She had scarcely entered when another woman also carrying a bundle came in too; and she was closely followed by a man who brought a bundle of his own. When each one saw the other two there, they all three burst into a laugh.

"Let the scrub woman be first!" cried she who had entered first. "Let the washerwoman be second, and let the undertaker's man be the third. Look here, old Joe. Ain't this a joke! If we haven't all three met here without meaning to!"

"You couldn't have met in a better place. You all come here often enough. What have you to sell? What have you got to sell?"

"Wait a minute, Joe, and you shall see."

Joe went down on his knees to make it easier to open the bundle, and dragged out a large, heavy roll of some dark stuff.

"What are these? Ah! Bed curtains!"

"Yes! Bed curtains! Don't drop that oil upon the blankets, now."

"*His* blankets?"

"Whose else's do you think? He isn't likely to catch a cold without 'em, I dare say. If he wanted to keep 'em after he was dead, the wicked old sinner, why wasn't he a better man in his lifetime? If he had been, he'd have had somebody to look after him when he died, instead of lying gasping out his last breath there, alone by himself. Ah! You can look through that shirt till your eyes ache, but you won't find a hole in it or a threadbare place. It's the best he had and a fine one too. They'd have wasted it by dressing him in it if it hadn't been for me."

Scrooge listened in fear.

"Spirit! I see, I see. What has happened to this unhappy man might happen to me! My life leads that way, now. Merciful heaven, what is this?"

The scene had changed, and now he almost touched a bare uncurtained bed. Pale moonlight fell upon this bed; and on it, unwatched and uncared for, was the body of the robbed, unknown man.

Just as suddenly the scene changed once more. The ghost conducted him to poor Bob Cratchit's house—where he had visited before—and they found the mother and children seated around the fire.

The mother laid her sewing upon the table and put her hand up to her face. "The color hurts my eyes," she said. "They're better again now. The candlelight makes them water, and I wouldn't show red eyes to your father when he comes home for the world. It must be nearly time for him now."

"Past it," Peter answered. "But I think he has walked a little slower than he used to these last few evenings, Mother."

"I have known him to walk with—I have known him to walk with Tiny Tim upon his shoulder very fast indeed."

"And so have I," cried Peter. "Often."

"And so have I," said another. They all had.

"But he was very light to carry, and his father loved him so, that it was no trouble—no trouble. But hush, now, there is your father at the door!"

She hurried out to meet him as Bob in his ragged white scarf came in. His tea was ready for him by the fire, and they all tried to be first to help him to it. Then the two young Cratchits got upon his knees, and each child laid a little cheek against his face as if to say, "Don't mind it, Father. Don't be sad!"

Bob acted very cheerful with them and spoke pleasantly to all the family. He looked at the new suit upon the table and praised the work and speed of Mrs. Cratchit and the girls. It would be ready in time for Tiny Tim to be buried in on Sunday, he said.

"Sunday! Then you went to the cemetery today, Robert?"

"Yes, my dear," he said. "I wish you could have gone. It would have done you good to see how green a place it is. But you'll see it often. I promised him that I would walk there on Sundays. My little, little child! My little child!"

He broke down all at once. He couldn't help it. He had loved Tiny Tim so!

"Spirit," said Scrooge, "something tells me that our visit is nearly over. Tell me who that man was with the covered face whom we saw lying dead."

The Ghost of Christmas Yet to Come took him to a deserted graveyard.

The spirit stood among the graves and pointed down to one.

"Before I move closer to that headstone to which you point, answer me one question. Are you showing me the things that *will* be, or are they only the things that *may* be?"

Still the ghost pointed downward to the grave by which it stood.

"A man's life may lead him down unhappy paths. But if he changes his life and becomes a better man, then he might have time to find happier paths to follow. Isn't that so, Spirit?"

The spirit was as silent as ever.

Scrooge crept towards it, trembling as he went. Following the finger, he read upon the stone his own name—Ebenezer Scrooge.

"Am I that man who lay upon the bed? No, Spirit! Oh no, no! Spirit! hear me! I am not the man I was. Because of this visit, I will never be that man again! Why show me this if I am past all hope? Tell me that by changing my life I may change these things you have shown me!"

For the first time the phantom lowered its hand.

"I will honor Christmas in my heart, and try to keep it all the year. I will live in the past, the present, and the future. The spirits of all three shall live within me. I will never forget the lessons that they teach. Oh, tell me I may erase away the writing on this stone!"

As he reached out to touch the dark robe, the phantom began to change. It shrunk, grew thin, and dwindled down into a bedpost.

Yes, and the bedpost was his own. The bed was his own, the room was his own. Best and happiest of all, there was still time left for him to change his life!

Outside, the church bells were ringing loudly. Running to the window, he opened it and stuck his head out. No fog, no mist, no night. It was a clear, bright, golden day.

"What's today?" cried Scrooge, calling downward to a boy in Sunday clothes.

"Today! Why Christmas day!"

"It's Christmas day! I haven't missed it. Do you know the butcher shop in the next street over at the corner?"

"I sure do."

"An intelligent boy! A very fine boy! Do you know whether they've sold the prize turkey that was hanging up there? Not the little prize turkey—the big one?"

"What, the one as big as me?"

"What a delightful boy! Yes, my boy!"

"It's hanging there now."

"Is it? Go and buy it. Go and tell them to bring it here. I'll tell them where to take it. Come back with the man, and I'll give you a shilling. Come back with him in less than five minutes, and I'll give you half a crown!"

The boy was off like a shot.

"I'll send it to Bob Cratchit's! He won't know who sent it. It's twice the size of Tiny Tim!"

He wrote down the address and went to open the street door to be ready for the butcher when he came. What a turkey it was! Scrooge had never seen such a bird, and he rubbed his hands with glee as he watched the man taking it to Bob Cratchit's.

Then Scrooge dressed himself in his very best clothes and at last got out into the streets. Walking with his hands behind him, Scrooge greeted everyone he met with a delighted smile. He looked so pleasant that people smiled back and said, "Good morning, sir! A Merry Christmas to you!"

And Scrooge often said afterwards, that of all the happy sounds he had ever heard, those were the happiest of all.

In the afternoon he walked to his nephew's house.

"Is your master at home, my dear?" said Scrooge to the girl who opened the door. "Nice girl! Very."

"Yes, sir."

"Where is he, my love?"

"He's in the dining room, sir, with the mistress."

"He knows me," said Scrooge. "I'll go on in, my dear."

"Fred! There's a gentleman to see you."

"Why, bless my soul!" cried Fred. "It's Uncle Scrooge!"

"I have come to dinner. Will you let me in, Fred?"

Let him in! Fred shook his hand warmly, and his wife kissed Scrooge on the cheek. He felt at home in five minutes. Nothing could be merrier. His niece looked just the same. So did Topper when *he* came. So did every one when *they* came. Wonderful party, wonderful games, wonderful happiness!

But he was early at the office next morning. If he could only be there first and catch Bob Cratchit coming in late! He had his heart set on it.

And he did it.

The clock struck nine. No Bob. A quarter past. No Bob. Bob was eighteen and a half minutes late. Scrooge sat with his door wide open that he might see him come in.

Bob's hat was off before he opened the door, his scarf too. He was on his stool in a jiffy writing away with his pen, trying to make up for those eighteen and a half minutes.

"Hello!" growled Scrooge, in his usual voice. "What do you mean by coming here at this time of day?"

"I am very sorry, sir. I know I am late."

"You are? Yes. I think you are. Step this way if you please."

"It's only once a year, sir. It won't happen again. I was making rather merry yesterday, sir."

"Now, I'll tell you what, my friend. I am not going to stand for this sort of thing any longer. And therefore," Scrooge continued, leaping from his stool so that Bob took two steps backward, "and, therefore, I am about to raise your salary!"

Bob trembled and got a little nearer to the door.

"A Merry Christmas, Bob!" said Scrooge. With a twinkle in his eyes, he clapped him on the back. "A merrier Christmas, Bob, my good fellow, than I have given you for many a year! I'll raise your salary, and help your family, and we will talk it over this very afternoon, Bob! Build up the fires, and buy a fresh bucket of coal before you dot another *i*, Bob Cratchit!"

Scrooge more than kept his word. He did it all, and much, much more. And to Tiny Tim, who did not die, he was a second father. He became as good a friend, as good a master, and as good a man as the old city had ever known. Some people laughed to see the change in him; but he was happy, and that was enough for him.

Scrooge had no further meetings with spirits, and it was always said of him that he knew how to keep Christmas as well as any man alive. May that be truly said of us, all of us! And so, as Tiny Tim observed:

GOD BLESS US, EVERY ONE!

A MERRY CHRISTMAS
AND
A HAPPY NEW YEAR
TO YOU

Published at Summerly's Home Treasury Office
12 Old Bond Street London

THE FIRST CHRISTMAS CARD

Christmas 1843 was a historic time in London. "A Christmas Carol," just published by Charles Dickens, was bringing a tender tear to the eyes of thousands of readers. And an English gentleman, Sir Henry Cole, was having an artist friend design a Christmas greeting (shown above) to send to his friends. It was to be the first Christmas card. The design, by John Calcott Horsley, was lithographed in black and white and then colored by hand. About a thousand copies were produced. It took 30 more years, however, for Christmas cards to become popular. They were first introduced in the United States in the late 1870s.

It is good to be children sometimes,
and never better
than at Christmas time.

CHARLES DICKENS

Those warm times shared
in past Decembers –
The mind still sees,
the heart remembers.

HADIN MARSHALL

Original paintings by Norman Rockwell
from the Hallmark Collections

Christmas is here,
Merry old Christmas,
Gift-bearing, heart-touching,
Joy-bringing Christmas,
Day of grand memories,
      king of the year!

WASHINGTON IRVING

Christmas Morning Comes Too Soon

Christmas morning
   comes too soon.
Anticipation's best.
The sugar- shivers of the Eve
Were wealthiest.

The pine-rise
   and the shining eyes,
The bounces and applause
Mixing in mosaic
   with gift and cake,
Tinsels, berry sauce,

Wrappings silver, golden, red,
And ginger-cooky things.
Anticipation's best: next, the
Rememberings.
          Gwendolyn Brooks

Sledding

Sledding
   and heading for spaces below,
Gliding
   and sliding across the new snow,
Slicing
   an icing of white on the hill,
Leaning,
   careening, avoiding a spill.
Racing
   to where the icy hill ends —
A boy and his sled
   become wintry friends.
          Judy Mahar

The Cock at Midnight

The cock at midnight
begins to crow,
for the green moonlight
on the powdery snow...

for a child who may wander
all but lost
in the silver forest,
the sifting frost,

listening, seeking
through ice and thorn
the kneeling cattle,
the Lord just born!
Florence Jacobs

Christmas Is Here!

Frost on the windowpane,
Carolers singing,
Snow falling gently,
And gay sleigh bells ringing,
Isn't it wonderful!
Christmas is here —
The gladdest and happiest
Time of the year!
Mary Dawson Hughes

The Yule Log

I like the idea of the Yule Log, the enormous block of
wood, carefully selected long before, and preserved
where it would be thoroughly dry, which burned on the
old-fashioned hearth....I like the festoons of holly on
the walls and windows; the dance under the mistletoe;
the gigantic sausage; the baron of beef; the vast globe
of plum-pudding, the true image of the earth, flattened
at the poles. I like the idea of what has gone, and I can
still enjoy the reality of what remains.
Thomas Love Peacock

The Christmas Story

According to St. Luke

AND IT CAME TO PASS IN THOSE DAYS, THAT THERE WENT OUT A DECREE FROM CAESAR AUGUSTUS, THAT ALL THE WORLD SHOULD BE TAXED....AND ALL WENT TO BE TAXED, EVERY ONE INTO HIS OWN CITY.

AND JOSEPH ALSO WENT UP FROM GALILEE, OUT OF THE CITY OF NAZARETH, INTO JUDAEA, UNTO THE CITY OF DAVID, WHICH IS CALLED BETHLEHEM; (BECAUSE HE WAS OF THE HOUSE AND LINEAGE OF DAVID:) TO BE TAXED WITH MARY HIS ESPOUSED WIFE, BEING GREAT WITH CHILD.

AND SO IT WAS, THAT, WHILE THEY WERE THERE, THE DAYS WERE ACCOMPLISHED THAT SHE SHOULD BE DELIVERED.

AND SHE BROUGHT FORTH HER FIRSTBORN SON, AND WRAPPED HIM IN SWADDLING CLOTHES, AND LAID HIM IN A MANGER; BECAUSE THERE WAS NO ROOM FOR THEM IN THE INN.

AND THERE WERE IN THE SAME COUNTRY SHEPHERDS ABIDING IN THE FIELD, KEEPING WATCH OVER THEIR FLOCK BY NIGHT.

AND, LO, THE ANGEL OF THE LORD CAME UPON THEM, AND THE GLORY OF THE LORD SHONE ROUND ABOUT THEM: AND THEY WERE SORE AFRAID.

Illustration by Fernando Casini

AND THE ANGEL SAID UNTO THEM, FEAR NOT: FOR, BEHOLD, I BRING YOU GOOD TIDINGS OF GREAT JOY, WHICH SHALL BE TO ALL PEOPLE. FOR UNTO YOU IS BORN THIS DAY IN THE CITY OF DAVID A SAVIOUR, WHICH IS CHRIST THE LORD. AND THIS SHALL BE A SIGN UNTO YOU; YE SHALL FIND THE BABE WRAPPED IN SWADDLING CLOTHES, LYING IN A MANGER. AND SUDDENLY THERE WAS WITH THE ANGEL A MULTITUDE OF THE HEAVENLY HOST PRAISING GOD, AND SAYING,

Glory to God in the highest, and on earth Peace, Goodwill toward men!

I am thinking of you today because it is Christmas,
and I wish you happiness. And tomorrow, because it
will be the day after Christmas, I shall still wish you
happiness. I may not be able to tell you about it
every day, because I may be far away or we may be
very busy. But that makes no difference — my thoughts
and my wishes will be with you just the same.
Whatever joy or success comes to you will make me
glad. Clear through the year —
  I wish you the Spirit of Christmas.

Henry van Dyke

Letter to a Friend

I salute you. I am your friend and my love for you goes deep. There is nothing I can give you which you have not got; but there is much, very much, that, while I cannot give it, you can take.

No Heaven can come to us unless our hearts find rest in today. Take Heaven! No peace lies in the future which is not hidden in this present little instance. Take Peace! The gloom of the world is but a shadow. Behind it, yet within our reach, is Joy. There is radiance and glory in the darkness, could we but see — and to see we have only to look. I beseech you to look.

Life is so generous a giver, but we, judging its gifts by their covering, cast them away as ugly or heavy or hard. Remove the covering and you will find beneath it a living splendor, woven of love, by wisdom, with power.

Welcome it, grasp it, and you touch the Angel's hand that brings it to you. Everything we call a trial or a sorrow or a duty, believe me, that Angel's hand is there; the gift is there, and the wonder of an overshadowing presence. Our joys too: be not content with them as joys. They too conceal diviner gifts.

Life is so full of meaning and purpose, so full of beauty — beneath its covering — that you will find earth but cloaks your heaven. Courage then to claim it, that is all! But courage you have, and the knowledge that we are pilgrims together, wending through unknown country, home.

And so, at this Christmas time, I greet you. Not quite as the world sends greetings, but with profound esteem and with the prayer that for you, now and forever, the day breaks, and the shadows flee away.

Fra Giovanni

FAVORITE HOLIDAY RECIPES

Old-Fashioned Plum Pudding

½ lb. currants	½ lb. seeded raisins
½ lb. brown sugar	½ lb. seedless raisins
3 cups coarse bread crumbs	½ lb. suet, chopped
6 eggs, beaten until light	1½ teaspoons cinnamon
1½ teaspoons nutmeg	¾ teaspoon allspice
½ teaspoon cloves	½ cup white wine
½ cup brandy (and more)	¼ lb. finely cut citron
	¼ lb. candied orange peel

Place all ingredients in a large bowl. Mix well using both hands. Pack into one large melon mold or two medium-sized ones. (Coffee cans make a good substitute for molds.) Cover tightly. Place on a trivet in a deep-well cooker or large kettle filled with enough water to come ⅔ up sides of mold. Boil 4 to 8 hours — the longer the better. Remove pudding from mold and allow to cool while cleaning mold thoroughly. Replace cooled pudding in mold and prick pudding with knife or knitting needle. Sprinkle with 3 tablespoons of brandy. Repeat this process at the end of one week. Keep pudding covered so it will not dry out. When ready to serve, reheat in kettle as before, boiling for 2 hours. Remove from mold, pour 2 tablespoons brandy over it, touch with lighted match and carry it, flaming, to your waiting guests.

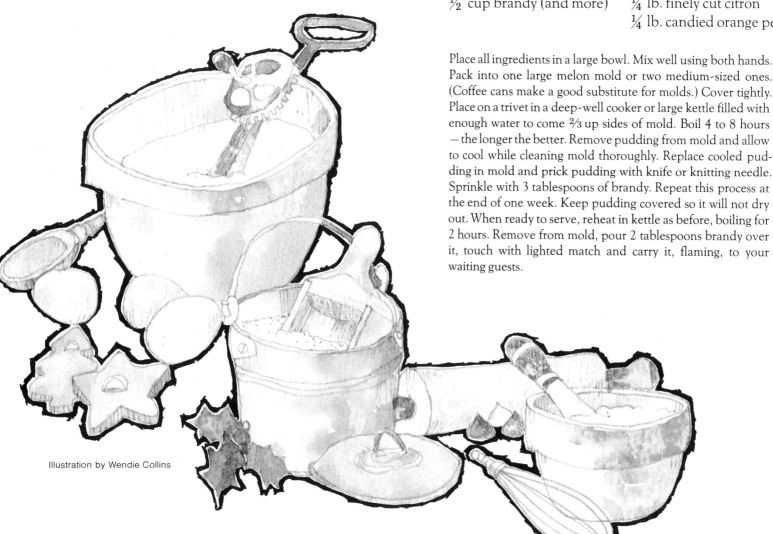

Illustration by Wendie Collins

Christmas Eggnog

6 egg yolks	2 pints heavy whipping cream
½ pint rum	6 tablespoons confectioners' sugar
½ pint brandy	1 cup granulated sugar

Beat egg yolks well, add granulated sugar. Add liquor, then slowly add enough cream to make a pale lemon color. Whip remaining cream and add confectioners' sugar. Fold into egg mixture. Grate a little nutmeg on top.

Sparkling Christmas Punch

4 oz. lemon juice	3 oz. grenadine or
4 oz. pineapple juice	maraschino syrup
3 oz. fruit cordial	1 bottle white wine
8 oz. brandy	2 bottles chilled champagne

Mix all ingredients except champagne over ice in a bowl. Add the sparkling champagne just before serving. Garnish bowl with fruit slices and strawberries. Makes 32 servings.

Cranberry Nut Bread

3 cups sifted flour	1 beaten egg
4 teaspoons baking powder	1 cup milk
1 teaspoon salt	2 tablespoons melted butter
1 cup granulated sugar	1½ cups cranberries, sliced
Grated peel of one orange	1 cup chopped pecans

Sift together flour, baking powder, salt and sugar; add grated orange peel. Combine egg, milk and melted butter. Gradually stir in flour mixture. Add sliced cranberries and pecans. Pour into greased and floured loaf pan. Bake 1 hour at 350°. Cool thoroughly, wrap in foil and refrigerate before slicing. This bread makes delicious sandwiches with butter or creamed cheese filling.

Christmas Butter Cookies

1 lb. butter	4 eggs
2 cups granulated sugar	4 cups sifted flour

Cream sugar and butter together. Add eggs one at a time, mixing between each one. Work in flour. Chill batter for 2 hours. Roll out batter until about ¼ to ½ inch thick and cut out in desired designs. When ready to cook, brush cookies with beaten egg and sprinkle with almonds, sugar or silver dragées. Bake in moderate (350°-375°) oven for about 15 minutes. When cool, they may be frosted and decorated further.

Stuffed Dates

4½ cups sifted confectioners' sugar
⅔ cup sweetened condensed milk
¼ teaspoon salt
1½ teaspoons vanilla
¼ teaspoon almond extract
1½ lbs. whole pitted dates

Slowly add 4 cups of the sugar to the milk, blending well. Mix in the salt and extracts. Sprinkle the remaining ½ cup of sugar on a board and knead the fondant until smooth and creamy, working in the sugar. Wrap in foil and let it sit in the refrigerator for a day. Then stuff the dates and top them with walnut halves. This will make enough fondant to fill 7 to 8 dozen dates.

Olde Wassail

1 quart ale	Grated lemon peel
Nutmeg	3 eggs
Ginger	4 oz. granulated sugar (moistened)
	1 quart rum or brandy

Heat ale almost to boiling. Stir powdered ginger, grated nutmeg and grated lemon peel into it. Beat eggs with sugar while ale is heating. Put hot ale, eggs and sugar in one pitcher, and 1 quart of rum or brandy in another. Turn ingredients from one pitcher into another until mixture becomes smooth. Then pour into a holly-wreathed bowl and serve hot.

Hot Buttered Rum

½ oz. maple syrup
⅓ oz. lemon juice
1 oz. Jamaica rum

Pour ingredients into pre-heated mug or hot-drink glass. Fill balance of glass with hot water. Float ½ pat butter on top and sprinkle with nutmeg or cinnamon.

Favorite Family Recipes

Memories and Traditions